Table of Content

Copywrite Notice:

Introduction

Are you stuck?

Stuck in the same job, same company, same coworkers – and the world moves on.

No you are not alone.

There is a paradigm shift in how we work, how companies hire/fire and what to expect in a white collar job. Cost cutting, outsourcing, offshoring are the new buzz words.

When you look beyond the new globalization hype and the new work paradigm you will find that time tested techniques still matter. Career management is still a discipline that one needs to learn and execute upon. Selling your capabilities, creating a reputation, networking and mentoring are some of the concepts that one must leverage in any environment to enhance their career progression.

This eGuide is designed to educate, enlighten and provide guidance on career management best practices, techniques and strategies. Read, learn, apply and move – basically get unstuck.

How to Read this eGuide

Chapter 1: The Big Picture - What truly is your calling in life? The first chapter involves some soul searching to identify your passion, your value alignment and where you want to be eventually.

Chapter2: Getting There – This chapter provides insight on how to create a career progression plan. The realization of this plan helps you accomplish your overall objective.

Chapter 3: To Stay or To Go – You have to evaluate your progress and take a hard look at your current situation. Are you making progress or stagnating? If your progress is stalling – you need to consider your options.

Chapter 4: Keeping Up – The final chapter helps you understand tools and techniques that can feel the momentum going. You see the final objective but need help sustaining the tempo.

I - The Big Picture

Understanding the WHY

Yes there is a lot that has happened in the last few years. Whole industries have changed (automobiles), companies have disappeared (Anderson Consulting), markets have appeared (mobile computing), benefits have vanished (pension plans) and new workers have asserted themselves (Indian offshoring).

But beyond what is happening around you, there are reasons which are centered on you that may be holding you back. Consider the following –

The Comfort Zone

It takes substantial time and effort investment before we get comfortable in a job. Ironically, by the time we get comfortable we also stop or reduce the professional growth associated with that assignment. It's human nature to resist change but in this ever-changing global IT environment - change is inevitable. If you stay in your comfort zone for too long you risk becoming obsolete.

Personal Accountability

We can blame the company, the environment, project politics, management structure ... but ultimately it is your career. No one is more concerned about your career than you are. Your manager and company have an obligation to support you in your career endeavors but eventually you are responsible. You have to take responsibility for fixing the situation, changing it and moving on.

Self-Investment

Putting in 40hr at work may not be enough to move in the right direction. We live in changing times where we need to constantly review and upgrade our marketability. You make yourself marketable by investing in yourself through professional training, certifications, relationships, accomplishments, experiences etc. You have to look at where you are and where the market is headed in terms of technology, current trends, demographics and then define personal investment goals. It is work above and beyond the routine 40hrs but that is what it takes to get ahead.

Choice

Many of us are fortunate to live in an environment where we have the freedom to choose. There are constraints and limitations to consider but often we use them as a convenient excuse to not make the hard choices in life. We have to keep in mind that the choices we make today have implications that may last a lifetime. It's your life, your career and you are in charge - make the right and often times the tough choice to enjoy a fulfilling career.

What is a career path?

> If you don't know where you are going, any road will do – Anonymous

A roadmap! That is what a career path is. Generally when you start in any professional career you have to learn the breadth of your environment. And then you pick your options and tend to add depth to your skill repertoire.

During the formative years, you learn the industry components, business functions and thereby the specialization options. For example, in IT the following core functions exist
- **Management** – Generally a discipline where you are accountable for delivery of some product/service with the help of a pool of resources, using appropriate tools and processes.
- **Sales** – A function where you sell your companies products or services to clients/customers.
- **Business** – Understand the core business functions, translate them for IT enablement and support process optimization.
- **Technology** – Understanding the hardware, software, architecture and anything else which makes the IT systems function.

A new entrant in IT will learn about the above job functions and play roles in maybe different capacities. During these early years it is important to broaden your horizons and get a taste of the different options available.

After some experience in your field comes the time when one needs to pick a career path and focus on specialization. This entails charting a roadmap to your eventual goal state role. The roadmap defines the steps needed to traverse this journey and achieve your objective.

What makes you tick?

Passion! That is what should make you tick. If you love it, enjoy it, dig it – then go for it. Hopefully what you love to do also kicks back a paycheck.

Sometimes it is the reverse. We work to get a paycheck and then wonder where passion fits into this sequence. No easy answers here but when you think big (which is what this section is about) think about what do you really want to accomplish in life.

To be tremendously successful in life you have to be driven. And that insane drive comes when you are pursuing your dream. Look around and observe the passion and drive that industry leaders project. Life becomes a drag when your heart is not into it. An average career spans almost 40 years – wouldn't you want those 40 years to be the most exciting and wonderful years of your life.

"If you love what you do, you'll never work another day in your life" - Confucius

While you are contemplating what makes you tick – check out Steve Job's commencement speech at Stanford University - "Stay Hungry, Stay Foolish"[1].

---

[1] http://news-service.stanford.edu/news/2005/june15/jobs-061505.html

Value Alignment

> "To work in an organization the value system of which is unacceptable to a person, or incompatible with it, condemns the person both to frustration and to nonperformance." – Peter Ducker in <u>Managing Oneself</u>[2]

When contemplating career growth and progression, value alignment becomes a key concept that one needs to seriously consider. We have very different personalities and appreciate different things in life. When making career choices you need to consider cultural and value similarities between you and the prospective employer.

Consider the culture difference between a small company versus a giant like Walmart. How about difference in work ethic at Google or a startup? What these examples illustrate are different cultural attributes that organizations exhibit. Since you will be swimming in this pond for a while – make sure you like the shape, size, temperature and color of the pond.

Assess you career options and prospective employer on these lines
- **Size:** What do you prefer - small fish in a small pond or small fish in a large pond (If you are large fish – pond size is still relevant!)
- **Speed:** Think decision making and change. Done, next, move … does your head spin or do you get a rush?
- **Tempo:** High pressure, high stress, make or break – adrenaline junkie!
- **Footprint:** Local or global – love to travel and see the world.
- **People:** Who do you like to hang with - Baby Boomers, Gen x, Gen y, Millennia …
- **Hierarchy:** One-on-one with your manager at the corner bar or it is scheduled by the administrative assistant 2 months in advance in the main conference room.
- **Progressive:** Looking for 6 months of paternity leave?

You get the drift. It's almost like getting married. You are marrying your job but the family (in this case the company) is part of the deal. Think hard before you say – I do.

---

[2] http://harvardbusinessonline.hbsp.harvard.edu/b01/en/common/item_detail.jhtml?id=4444

A classic case of culture clash was the short tenure (10 months) of Julie Roehm at Walmart as their marketing executive. An excerpt from Businessweek[3] -

---

Still, Roehm recalls friends looking at her "like I was crazy" for taking the job. And from the moment she arrived at Wal-Mart on Feb. 6, 2006, Roehm recognized that fitting in would be harder than she had imagined. This wasn't Chrysler. And the Wal-Mart headquarters, with its windowless offices and gray walls, was hardly inspiring for a woman unafraid of a little color. One of the first things Roehm did was paint her office chartreuse with chocolate-brown trim. That may have been her first mistake—and it's revealing that Wal-Mart, in its response to Roehm's suit, says she is free to collect "a step ladder and paint supplies" left behind after she was dismissed.

Some new hires would keep a low profile and spend their first 100 days listening. That's not Roehm's style. "I get overly excited," she acknowledges. "I wanted to hit the ground running. Go, go, go." No one told her to back off; that's not the Wal-Mart way. Even though everyone was "super nice" and said things like "thanks for participating," Roehm heard from her own staff that "you shouldn't be doing" things like planning skits for the annual meeting."

Where do you want to be?

And finally – where do you want to be. Eventually! In other words think long term. Think 20 years out. Can you see yourself in this job, with this company, in this industry?

This big picture stuff should ideally formalize your goal state. The soul searching, the industry outlook, the global economy, the shifting weather patterns – when you mix it all up – what do you end up with? Bulls-eye!

You have a goal in mind. Now go get it!

---

[3] http://www.businessweek.com/magazine/content/07_07/b4021076.htm?chan=rss_topStories_ssi_5

II - Getting There

Managing your Career

What you do everyday at work has an impact on your career. You interactions, presentation, communication and work product are all under constant scrutiny. To effectively manage your career you have to pursue a top down approach. Your overall career objectives become the basis for formulating an annual plan - what do you want to accomplish this year?

Annual plan

An annual plan is usually implemented by most companies and probably you do one every year. If it is dull and boring with 50 objectives you "*inherit*" that have no inkling to what you do – despair not. An annual plan can be a useful career management tool and here are some suggestions to reenergize your annual plan.

- **Is it about you?**
  That is the first question you need to address. If **your** annual plan does not address your career growth then there is an obvious problem. Keep the 50 generic rolled down objectives but create a 3-5 specific objectives that you want to achieve.

- **Does it fit the bigger objective?**
  Make sure these specific objectives address components of your long term strategic vision. If your long term objective is a senior project management position, your annual goals should support that view. Lateral learning that creates breadth and specialization that creates depth should both be addressed in your annual plan.

  This article[4] in Wall Street Journal reviews career growth strategies where senior executives took perceived demotions to learn the business (lateral growth) before leveraging that growth to propel their career.

---

[4] http://online.wsj.com/article/SB119619863214505610.html?mod=fpa_mostpop

▪ Is it realistic?

To be achievable, the plan should be realistic. You have to assess the company status, organizational aptitude and overall a reasonable progression rate for your career. Opportunities have to exist or be created, you have to learn and grow, and unforeseen circumstances have to be considered. That does not mean – aim lower but aim for a pragmatic plan.

▪ Is it measurable?

Like any plan – you need quantifiable progress points to ascertain progress. Training is easy to track but career growth is harder to quantify. To measure career progress, think in terms of number of people who you manage, span of control, budget accountability, annual targets etc.

▪ Review and review again and …

An annual plan defined early in the year and then forgotten for the rest of the year does not serve its true purpose. An annual plan is a living document which should form the basis for your assignments, training and annual growth. The plan should be regularly reference and revised as needed.

Check the reference section for a sample annual plan.

Assignment plan

Each assignment you undertake should fulfill an objective that ties back to your annual plan. Plus an assignment plan allows you to create a written agreement with your lead/manager around your assignment role, objectives and review criteria. Key components of an assignment plan include

▪ Each assignment makes a difference

Every assignment you undertake adds or takes away from your career pursuit. It's like building blocks. Each block makes a difference. First rule of assignment planning is – have a written assignment plan because it makes a difference.

▪ Role & deliverable definition

What is your role on this project and what is expected from you in terms of deliverables? This is the key question which the assignment plan needs to capture. Consider this definition to be a contract between you and the project. The more descriptive and detailed the assignment – the less chance of misunderstood expectations.

Grading
What will get you an A grade versus a D? Expectations without tangible results tend to be subjective. Getting performance metrics defined upfront makes your performance review more objective. You also understand upfront what is expected from you to achieve the high grades. If the bar is set too high or too low – this is the time to negotiate.

Review
Similar to an annual plan, an assignment plan is a living document. As project requirements or job functions change – the assignment plan needs to reflect that change.

As an example consider hiring a plumber to remodel your bathroom. Before you hire the plumber you will create a written contract that will detail the planned work, output, rates, payment schedule etc. Midway, if you change your requirements – expect the contract to be revisited also. An assignment plan is a similar contract between you and your project – it is there to help both sides objectively articulate expectations, roles, deliverables and results. Remember a contract is subject to negotiations to ensure both parties are entering into a win-win engagement. This is your opportunity to negotiate your assignment and expectations. If this job is not for you – now is the time to consider other assignments and options.

Periodic review

All the paper you have created so far and filed away has served some purpose in aligning your career progression. But the task is not done and those pieces of paper still have a role to play. You keep your annual plan and assignment plan in perspective by regularly and periodically reviewing your performance. It's always better to have more opportunities to work on your deficiencies rather than less. And the sooner you can start to fix your deficiencies the better for your career progression.

- **Monthly one-on-one with manager**
  Constant feedback! Think about it – if at every step of the way you were told – right or wrong – how easy life would be. A one-one-one with your manager is an opportunity to do just that – figure out how many rights and how many wrongs.

  Some key pointers for effective one-on-ones
  - Schedule them in advance on a recurring basis and stick with them.
  - Spend 30 minutes to an hour in each one-on-one
  - Use a written status report that covers the period from your last review as the basis for this meeting
  - Get honest feedback on your performance (use the grading scheme defined in the assignment plan to get objective feedback)
  - Define action items - both for you and your manager
  - Review pending actions items

- **One-on-one with peers and other managers**
  One-on-one or just a meeting is also merited with peers and managers who are involved on your project. These meetings are opportunities to expand your feedback loop and get perspective from different angles. Your boss is happy but is the customer happy?

One-on-ones not only provide a means to get feedback, they are excellent means to build relationships. Since you benefit greatly (like you do with many things I mention in this eGuide), make the effort to reach out and interact with as many critical players as possible.

Assignment Closure

We know we should do it – but often neglect to get it done. The final review allows you to close the loop on that assignment. If you have been diligent in your one-on-ones hopefully the final review should not be very extensive.

Work with your manager to incorporate this feedback into your assignment plan. If done right you should end up with a written assignment plan, your periodic performance on that assignment and a final assessment.

Year End Review

Ideally this should be a non-event! After all this is the accumulation of all that has transpired over the last year. If the annual plan was maintained, each assignment performance documented and 360degree feedback solicited throughout the year – then what is left.

The year-end review should be an opportunity to review the year at a macro level. Revisit the annual plan and assess accomplishment against that. The new annual plan will evolve from the year-end review.

Special Note

I cannot emphasize enough the need to create a paper trail of your performance from your managers, peers and clients. Consultants working away from their home office and employees with matrix reporting can generally leverage such feedback (written and objective) when year-end performance reviews are conducted. It is very hard to ignore a documented paper trail of excellent performance.

Creating a Brand

A brand symbolizes the organization, reflects its value and creates credibility. Companies spend millions of dollars creating a brand and even more money defending their brands. Once established, a brand is a powerful symbol of the organization. Think about Nike, McDonald's, Coke, Starbucks, Nestle – strong brands that speak for themselves.

As individuals in the corporate environment – we are also playing the same game as these bigger organizations. Our sphere of influence is much smaller but it's the same game - establishing credibility, showcasing your values and building competencies. As you work and establish yourself in any company you build your own brand.

Your brand reflects who you are, how you perform, how you interact and how you deliver. To establish a great brand you have to
- Be aware of who you want to be
- Focus on creating the brand (self-promotion or active marketing)
- Deliver on your commitments and
- Nurture your brand

Awareness about this concept is the starting point. You may see this as a branding exercise or a credibility building effort – the end result is the same. When you start – you are an unknown variable and over time you establish your brand/credibility.

Review the section on "active marketing" to get some pointers on how to build your brand. It is primarily a self promotion and networking exercise. This needs to be backed up by actual delivery, commitment and a value set that you embody. Just talk and no substance will only take you so far.

Consistent branding is the name of the game. It needs to be a part of you – how you function and work. This is not a once in a while exercise but a way of interacting, delivering value and reinforcing your brand. Keep your brand fresh and the marketing campaign active.

Active Marketing

Every day at work you have opportunities to market your skills, articulate your contributions and seek the right opportunities. This is called active marketing. Active marketing is a cornerstone of progressive career management and is critical for career growth, compensation/merit increase and recognition. Specifically, active marketing entails professional, organizational, community and domain marketing.

Professional Marketing

Professional marketing happens at the workplace. At work you have opportunities to create a positive impact with your client, peers and management team everyday. You are evaluated everyday at work – make sure you put forth your best effort. Use appropriate opportunities to expound your accomplishments, create a broad network of professional engagements and make sure you are known entity in your team.

Organizational Marketing

The organization you work for will have an organizational structure. You have to learn that structure and make the right people connections. Just knowing your boss is not good enough. You have to seek out mentors and advisors within your organization and also have active relationships with people above and around you. This is a small world and knowing how your organization works and who has influence can help you in the long term.

Community Marketing

Being part of a community should also be an opportunity to seek out and communicate your competencies and skills. Actively marketing your success and credibility can help create awareness about you – again it's the network which counts.

Domain Marketing

There are ample technical and professional organizations which meet on a regular basis – host sessions and provide networking opportunities. Another venue to showcase your skills (seek out a speaking opportunity) and meet people from your profession.

Make an effort to actively market your skills and competencies across various forums – team, organization, client setting, community and professional organizations – as often as possible. This is a long term strategy which helps create a broad network and creates awareness about you.

Marketing Strategies

Communication – Nothing gets the message out about you if there is no communication. Listed below are some communication opportunities that should be leveraged as often as possible

- **Group meetings**: Speak up! Let your presence be known in meetings. I am not espousing speaking for the sake of speaking but find something relevant to contribute in a meeting. If you are shy or insecure about your contribution – start by setting a goal to say at least one thing in each meeting. As your comfort level improves, become more vocal and involved..
- **One-on-ones:** Make it a point to buy someone lunch every week. Client manager, peer, subordinate, specialist – anyone who is associated with your project and team. A $10/15 investment gives you 60 minutes of face time with an exceptional individual. This is an opportunity to understand their world, their perspective, their view on the industry and also allows you to articulate your background and competencies to them.
- **Public speaking:** Not the easiest thing to do but if you are up to it, public speaking puts you in front of a lot of people. Ask for opportunities where you can participate in a limited capacity to get your feet wet. Go from there.

An excellent resource to develop public speaking confidence is Toastmasters International[5]. A nonprofit organization with nearly 220,000 members in 11,300 clubs in 90 countries, offering a proven – and enjoyable! – way to practice and hone communication and leadership skills.

---

[5] http://www.toastmasters.org/

Mentors – Mentors are individuals who because of their position and perspective can provide you with valuable feedback. Mentors are relationships you have to intentionally cultivate. Pick mentors from different walks of life. In other words all your mentors don't need to part of your professional network. Community leaders can be mentors, successful entrepreneurs can be mentors, and business leaders can be mentors – anyone with a perspective that can make you a better employee, employer or manager can be your mentor.

Status reporting – Often considered a chore, this communication mechanism can be an effective marketing tool. A status report gives you a means to communicate with your manager on a regular basis. It achieves two important objectives – provides a means to get your message across and is documented.

This is an opportunity to showcase your accomplishments, successes and issues you face. If you keep your manager in the dark – you miss both the opportunity to highlight your accomplishments and actively address issues. Both these items can be detrimental to your career growth.

Check out the sample status report in the appendix for insights into how to write an effective status report.

Case Study

Bob is a consultant working at the client site. He has a good rapport with the client manager and he likes this assignment. Bob is expecting a good raise at the end of year because his client manager is happy and generally says good things about Bob's performance.

Year End - At the end of the year Bob gets a below average raise. Bob is surprised and frustrated. When he communicates his frustration his company states that his skill set is stagnating, the client account has not grown and the feedback from the client partner has been average.

Problem - So what happened in this situation? Bob limited his exposure to the client manager who although happy with Bob's work is not influential enough in the organization. Bob did not confirm his expectations on that account with his company. The company expected Bob to grow the account, gain some new skills and forge more relationships with the client.

Solution – Bob could have done the following to set himself up for success.

Defined an assignment plan with this company's management. This exercise would have clarified Bob's role and expectations from this assignment. Account growth and relationship building would have been discussed as objectives upfront thereby avoiding expectation surprises later.

Bob should have provided periodic status feedback to his company's management. This would have left a paper trail and also allowed Bob to regularly inform this company of his progress, accomplishment and possible issues.

Bob should have followed up his status reports by conducting regular one-on-one sessions with his company's management to confirm his progress and next steps.

Bob should have solicited regular feedback from this client manager and also reached out to the client partner to confirm that his assignment was truly adding value to the company. If any issues or lack of performance was indicated – Bob should have taken appropriate steps to fix that issue.

This case study articulates many aspects of client management, communication and reporting which eventually reduce the chances for mismatched expectations.

No surprise for anyone is the best strategy.

Delivering On Your Commitment

Nothing impacts your career progression more than your ability to deliver. You can communicate, build relationships, get feedback but if you cannot meet your commitments – there will implications. The following sections deal with some aspects of delivery.

Competency

Being competent in your job will take you far in your career - especially when competency is combined with the various career management strategies we have discussed. Competency is your ability to excel in your chosen vocation. To gain competency consider the following avenues

- **Education:** If you are involved in a technical line of work, some basic formal education in that field is almost essential. Consider community colleges, special classes or specialized education to get a good grounding in the basics.
- **Training:** You can always improve your skill set and investing in the right training should be high on your list. Your employer may support your training requirements but feel free to explore training options that support your career objectives.
- **Certification:** I am not a big proponent of collecting acronyms but if there are relevant certifications that can add to your repertoire of skills – go for it.
- **Experience:** Nothing teaches you better than experience. Focus and be diligent and there is a lot to learn on the job.
- **Teachers:** Learn from others as much as you can. You can learn what to do and also what not to do. Keep your eyes and ears open, reach out to people and learn from them.

Integrity

Nothing will kill your career faster than dishonesty and unethical behavior. Just look around and see how many CEOs have been ousted for cheating, unethical behavior and fraud. Employers, clients, coworkers and subordinates all appreciate honesty, integrity, values and compassion.

Who you are is always reflected in your work. Consider the following situations which reflect on your values.

- **Fairness** - Are you willing to openly and fairly acknowledge credit where it is due?
- **Loyalty** - Are you seeking the best for your project and company?
- **Loyalty** - Are you investing in your team's growth and maturity?
- **Courage** - Are you upfront about project risks and issues?
- **Courage** - Do you have the courage and resolve to face tough situations?
- **Responsibility** - Are you willing to resolve challenges or are more eager to find a scapegoat?
- **Leadership** - Are you there for your team, project and company?

- **Trust** – Do your team members discuss relevant issues/challenges with you?
- **Integrity** – When you make a commitment do you always deliver?

People Growth

People make all the difference in any business. And a hallmark of success is investing in the people around you. Investing in people includes the following
- **Acknowledgement** – Acknowledging positive contribution goes a long way towards encouraging engagement and improves morale.
- **Challenge** – Growth is only possible when people have options and challenges. Support growth by creating challenging opportunities for you staff.
- **Investment** – Your time and effort investment is required to support people growth.

Follow-up

If you make a promise – keep it. If you need to change your commitment – let the other party know. Follow-up and "close the loop". Always!

Blame it on multi-tasking, overflowing mailboxes, competing priorities but often we fail to "close the loop". Superior service mandates timely and relevant communication to keep the affected party updated on progress or issues. Consider the following example to reinforce this point.

Case I - You drop off your car for routine service. The repair shop provides you with a tentative pick-up time and confirms that it will call you once the repair is complete.

The whole day goes by and you don't get a call. When you call you find out that the car was ready for pick-up 4 hours ago. This is a classis case of follow-up not done right.

Case II – Your manager requests a report from you. You indicate that you will have the report ready for him in a couple of days.

You spend a week on the report and want to get it just right. Since the report is not perfect you have not forwarded it your boss. Another example of poor follow-up.

Providing an update after 2 days to your boss on the status of the report would have been prudent. Maybe what you had was sufficient and perfection was not merited. Maybe the report was urgent and needed to be completed immediately. Keep the communication channel open – follow-up on your promises and commitment.

The Art of Listening

"Do you listen or wait to talk?"

That is a very powerful question. We often fall into this trap - when getting your point across becomes more important than understanding the other persons perspective. As consultants, employees, leaders, managers and employers – we should pay more heed to what is being said. If you don't know what people want, what their needs are, what their requirements are – then how will you fulfill their needs.

And once you start listening you will realize that more is being said than the words hitting your ear drums. Body-language, assumptions, history, culture, personality all play a role in understanding what is being said.

> "The most important thing in communication is to hear what isn't being said" – Peter Ducker

Harvard Business Review[6] has some excellent articles on listening. Consider attending some classes on business communications offered by your company or the local university/community college. A search at Amazon.com will lead you to a wide array of resources related to communication and listening.

---

[6]
http://www.hbsp.harvard.edu/b01/en/search/searchResults.jhtml?userView=CORPORATE&Ntx=mode+mat challpartial&Ntk=main_search&N=0&Ntt=listening

III - To Stay or To Go

Every once in a while you get bitten by the "time to move" bug. It happens – better money, better opportunity, more or less challenge, passion, culture, boss, weather …

Look before you leap

It is still working for you?

This is a question you need to ask yourself once a year. Even if you think that you love your job – consider the following questions.
- Are you moving up in your career?
- Are you getting good raises?
- Are you getting along with your co-workers and managers?
- Are you learning something new?
- Do you believe in your company's vision?
- Are you gaining marketable skills?

If you don't like the answer to some of these questions – it does not necessarily mean you have to find a new job. It may mean you have to address some career progression issues where you are, change your attitude, gain some new skills, broaden your horizons or seek new options.

In the post Is Your Job Really That Bad?[7] I explore some tendencies we have to occasionally complain for the sake of complaining. When you reflect on what you have – maybe it's not that bad.

Career coach Marty Nemko reminds us that you can love your current job if you have the right perspective. An excerpt from his article[8]

> "Sometimes, finding career contentment is simply a matter of diving into whatever job is available"

---

[7] http://itglobalsourcing.blogspot.com/2007/10/is-your-job-really-that-bad.html
[8] http://www.kiplinger.com/columns/onthejob/archive/2007/job1205.html

Getting complacent and comfortable to the point where you are almost in denial is a bad position to be in. If you are unwilling to make a change (although you know you should) sooner or later someone else will make that decision for you. Look at where you are, what you have to offer, how are things working for you, where is the industry headed and decide - should you stay or should you go?

An essay by Ram Charan[9] on this subject is highly recommended if you are unsure about your current job. If you are suffering from the "golden handcuff" syndrome – you might want to check out these words of wisdom[10] from the Wall Street Journal.

When You Decide to Go – Just Go!

> A hot-shot manager put in his 2 weeks notice and top management freaked out. He was indispensable, the key player in a proposal the company was about to submit … basically a superstar who had to be retained. More money sealed the deal and the star decided to stay – for another 2 months before he finally quit.

When you put in your 2 weeks notice – you have exhausted all possibilities and moving on is the final step. For some, resignation may be the starting point to negotiate a better deal but in my view that is a folly. In such cases the employer loses trust in the employee, the employee's commitment is shaken and eventually the two part ways. You can't reconcile a marriage by threatening divorce.

To make it work – you have to pursue a 3 step strategy.

Step 1 – You: Are you doing what it takes to succeed? Are you eager, motivated and willing to take that extra step to make it happen? We can very easily fall in the entitlement mode – where we expect the promotion and the raise.

Step 2 – Company: Are you still in love with your company? Do you

---

[9] http://finance.yahoo.com/expert/article/companyknow/11896
[10] http://finance.yahoo.com/career-work/article/103982/When-a-High-Paying-Job-Keeps-You-Low

dig the culture, the style and the company vision? If there is a drifting apart of values, strategies and objectives – time to rethink your tenure.

Step 3 – Time: Sometimes you hit a rough patch. Bad assignments, bad bosses, personal issues – you just can't seem to catch a break. Give it some time. Work to resolve the issues. Seek opportunities, be an exemplary worker, give it your best.

Finally - whatever the reason, you have pursued all options to make it work for you and it has not. That may be the time to move to the next gig.

IV - Keeping Up

To sustain your career growth you have keep up with the market, upcoming trends and your skills.

Industry Trends

Where is your industry headed? That is where your company is headed (sooner or later) and by default you are also. Keeping up with industry trends allows you to take the initiative to retrain, retool and expand out into new areas before they become routine. To increase your market awareness consider

- **Professional organizations**
  Membership in local chapters of professional organizations is an excellent way to keep up with industry trends. Sign up to hear industry leaders speak, attend lunch/learn sessions and subscribe to their newsletter.

- **Trade journals**
  You can sign up for free trade journals which again are an excellent source of market trends, industry news, leadership interviews and career opportunities.

- **Symposiums and seminars**
  Attend one or two symposiums per year to hear about newest trends, products and service offerings. Symposiums and seminars are also an excellent networking opportunity.

Marketable Skills

You are eventually a commodity in the market and career progression has to always keep the market in view. You may be going places in your organization but if the market does not value those skills – you will have a tough time moving around. Don't limit your growth to your company only – make yourself appealing in the overall market.

Certification and Education

You get instant recognition and credibility by adding acronyms behind your name. Eventually the value you provide is a combination of your experience, education, skills and credentials. Investing in marketable certificates and education can help you get a leg-up in the market place.

Invest in soft skills

Public speaking, negotiation skills, strategic thinking and conflict management are some of the core soft skills that will always be beneficial to your career growth. Join coaching organizations, take some classes – keep up your learning in people management and communication.

Keeping Up with Globalization

The Role of the Global Manager – A Perspective
Managers are in demand - worldwide. This assertion is backed up by the observations being made in emerging markets like China and India and also developed markets like America, Europe and Japan. The global economy is firing on all cylinders and the need for managers with special skills is fast outpacing availability. This could mean an opportunity for you. To be an effective manager in today's economy you need - strong people management skills, sourcing skills and global experience.

People Management
The ability to manage people is an exceptional skill. This basic management trait has been a valuable skill in the past but the requirements are evolving with the times. Management skills now require - managing across locations, across cultures and quickly adapting to evolving technological changes. To be hot in this space - you need to acquire the requisite skills and experience to compete in the global marketplace.

Sourcing
Globalization is changing the way companies staff for key skills. More than proximity – it's about talent and skill (remember The World is Flat). Learning the mechanics of sourcing strategy, skill acquisition,

vendor management and global workforce management are the new challenges.

- ■ **Global Experience**

And finally to be truly up to speed on these trends and effective you have to have experienced the global phenomenon. Cultural differences, different work practices and the human dynamics are very different in different parts of the world. Getting global exposure gives you the first hand knowledge and experience you need to be a truly "hot" commodity in this market.

Good is Fine but Great is Better

The world is flat[11]. In other words it's a global economy, which opens the door for competition. Competition for talent, competition for efficiency and competition for price - irrespective of border, time zone and culture. In this context just being good is not good enough. To excel in this environment and to get to the next level requires new thinking and strategies. Consider the following strategies in this space.

Micro-specialization

To move beyond the basic level of competency, you have to focus on super-specialization. You have to excel at something by having total mastery and knowledge about the subject matter. Just being a programmer will not cut it because everyone is a programmer. What is needed is a certified, ratified and glorified language specialist. Find your niche and then specialize - stand out in the crowd!

Super Certify

As a marketing tool, there is no substitute for industry certification. A well known, respected certification can grant you instant credibility. Every field has relevant certifications - find the ones that apply to your industry and don't be shy to attach those acronyms to your name.

---

[11] http://www.thomaslfriedman.com/worldisflat.htm

Industry Presence

Are you a known quantity in your industry? Do you have published papers, leadership position in industry groups, presentations in conferences, a well read blog ... To be a key player in your field requires an industry presence that augments and enhances your brand. Be a leader in your field by establishing yourself beyond your current corporate boundary.

Share & Grow

Above and beyond technical competency, greatness is a people quality. Great people and leaders establish themselves by sharing knowledge, promoting talent, learning from others and investing in people. When you become a role model, the go-to guy, the sought after mentor, the trusted lieutenant - you have crossed the boundary from good to great.

In the new business environment, technical skills and generic roles are commodities. Commodities those are available globally and readily. Take the steps to learn, educate, grow and establish you at the next level. Don't just achieve, exceed!

Conclusion

Pumped up and ready to succeed. Hopefully that is the way you feel after reading this eGuide. These tips, techniques and strategies are after all just that – guidance. We have shown you the door, now it's up to you to open the door and discover your potential.

Believe in your abilities, apply these strategies and achieve success in your career progression. The only thing between today and the new tomorrow is YOU. You have the tools and the knowledge to make it happen – take control of your career and get unstuck!

How to buy "unstuck"

If you bought this copy of **Unstuck** – thank you and congratulations! I hope you found the strategies helpful and applicable to your situation. I would love to hear from you. Please email me at MarkRunta@yahoo.com.

If you would like to buy **Unstuck** – please visit Amazon.com to download or buy a copy. What does an official copy buy you?

- The latest copy of Unstuck with updated content and sections
- Discount on future eGuides and eBooks
- Free access to new section and chapters

Upcoming eGuides

- **Global Workplace** – Strategies and tips to compete in the global workplace and win
- **Offshoring 101** – Practical guidance to get started with offshoring
- **Welcome Team Lead** – Effective strategies to succeed as a team lead

References

Articles and Blog Posts on Career Management

- **Promotion – How to Make It Happen:**
  (http://itglobalsourcing.blogspot.com/2007/09/promotion-making-it-happen.html)
  A blog post that provides pointers on doing the right things to get a promotion. Don't wait for a promotion – make it happen.

- **When to Grow, When to Go:**
  (http://finance.yahoo.com/columnist/article/companyknow/11896)
  An excellent article by industry guru Ram Charan that shakes you out of your comfort zone and makes you answer some tough questions.

- **How to Get Ahead by Going Backward:**
  (http://online.wsj.com/article/SB119619863214505610.html?mod=fpa_mostpop)
  Wall Street Journal reviews strategies used by senior executives to broaden their skill sets to help their career progression.

- **What Makes Employees Stay Put**
  (http://online.wsj.com/article/SB119522712907495804.html?mod=SmallBusinessSmallBusinessLink_feature_articles)
  Wall Street Journal Small Business Section discusses strategies and options to motivate and retain employees.

- **Strategies for Career Change**
  (http://www.careerjournal.com/jobhunting/change/20050120-stevens.html) Career Journal discusses a four steps approach for changing careers.

- **When a High Paying Job Keeps You Low**
  (http://finance.yahoo.com/career-work/article/103982/When-a-High-Paying-Job-Keeps-You-Low)
  The "golden handcuff" syndrome. When the money is good but the job is not – you have some choices to consider.

- **Do What You Love and Starve**
  (http://www.kiplinger.com/columns/onthejob/archive/2007/job1205.html) Prudent advice from a career coach on rethinking the notion of "follow your passion".

- **Stay Hungry, Stay Foolish**
  (http://news-service.stanford.edu/news/2005/june15/jobs-061505.html) Inspirational commencement speech by Steve Jobs that touches on passion, destiny and opportunity. A must read!

- **Saying more by saying less**
  (http://www.slantsixcreative.com/2007/12/04/saying-more-by-saying-less/) A blog post on when it is wise to say less and listen more.

- **Five Steps to Negotiating a Raise**
  (http://www.kiplinger.com/columns/starting/archive/2006/st1101.htm) Kiplinger.com provides some strategies to consider when negotiating a raise.

Books, Blogs and Websites

- **Peter F. Ducker's _Management Challenges for the 21st Century_** (Book)

  No single person has influenced the course of business in the 20th century as much as Peter Drucker. He practically invented management as a discipline in the 1950s, elevating it from an ignored, even despised, profession into a necessary institution that "reflects the basic spirit of the modern age." Now, in _Management Challenges for the 21st Century_, Drucker looks at the profound social and economic changes occurring today and considers how management--not government or free markets--should orient itself to address these new realities.

- **Tom Friedman's _The World is Flat: A Brief History of the Twenty-first Century_** (Book)

  Friedman is a Pulitzer Prize-winning _New York Times_ columnist and best-selling author who gives a bold, timely, and surprising picture of the state of globalization in the twenty-first century.

- **Marcus Buckingham & Curt Coffman First, Break All the Rules: What the World's Greatest Managers Do Differently** (Book)

  Marcus Buckingham and Curt Coffman expose the fallacies of standard management thinking in _First, Break All the Rules: What the World's Greatest Managers Do Differently_. In seven chapters, the two consultants for the Gallup Organization debunk some dearly held notions about management, such as "treat people as you like to be treated"; "people are capable of almost anything"; and "a manager's role is diminishing in today's economy." "Great managers are revolutionaries," the authors write. "This book will take you inside the minds of these managers to explain why they have toppled conventional wisdom and reveal the new truths they have forged in its place."

- **Penelope Trunk's The Brazen Careerist** (Blog)
  (http://blog.penelopetrunk.com/)

  Penelope Trunk writes career advice for a new generation of workers. She explains why old advice - like pay your dues, climb the ladder, and don't have gaps in your resume - is outdated and irrelevant in today's workplace. She has a reputation for giving advice that is counterintuitive but effective, like take long lunches, ignore people who steal your ideas, and stop vying for a promotion.

- **Ram Charan's What Every Company Should Know** (Book)

Ram Charan is a highly acclaimed business advisor, speaker, and author who has coached some of the world's most successful CEOs. For 35 years, he's worked behind the scenes at companies like GE, Bank of America, DuPont, Home Depot, 3M, and Verizon.

Career Journal.com

Wall Street Journal's online career management website provides career advice, expert opinion, job-hunting advice, salary and hiring information.

Samples & Other Reference Material

Engagement Assessment

Answer these 12 questions to validate your engagement level in your current job. If you don't answer positively to all these questions – red flags should start to go up.

- Do I know what is expected of me at work?
- Do I have the materials and equipment I need to do my work right?
- At work, do I have the opportunity to do what I do best everyday?
- In the last seven days, have I received recognition or praise for doing good work?
- Does my supervisor or someone at work seem to care about me as a person?
- Is there someone at work who encourages my development?
- At work, do my opinions seem to count?
- Does the mission/purpose of my company make me feel my job is important?
- Are my co-workers committed to doing quality work?
- Do I have a best friend at work?
- In the past six months, has someone at work talked to me about my progress?
- This last year, have I had the opportunity at work to learn and grow?

Based on the best selling book –
"First Break All The Rules, What The World's Greatest Managers Do Differently"
by *Marcus Buckingham and Curt Coffman*.

Sample Annual Plan

Number of objectives is limited. A good number is 3 to 5.

Annual Plan (2007) for Mark Runta

Career Objectives #1:
Effectively manage and deliver the XYZ project in 2007. Parameters to track successful delivery include

Exceeds Grade: Project variance limited to 5% for agreed scope and duration.
Meets Grade: Project variance limited to 10% for agreed scope and duration.
Fails Grade: Project variance exceeds 10% of budget.

Objectives cover different aspects of career growth, namely competency, training and resource management

Career Objective # 2:
Get PMP certified and provide guidance to junior staff in learning key project management concepts.

Exceeds Grade: Pass certification in 1 attempt with no special training.
Meets Grade: Pass certification in 1 attempt with paid training.
Fails Grade: Fail certification test.

Career Objective # 3:
Educate, train and mentor team. Limit attrition, provide growth opportunities and create a backup plan.

Exceeds Grade: Zero attrition, team morale and growth high (as accessed by 360 degree review).
Meets Grade: Low attrition and reasonable morale.
Fails Grade: High attrition and bad morale.

Each objective should have measurable achievement criteria.

Sample Status Report

Accomplishment
- List accomplishments for this period.
- Accomplishment definition should be descriptive and relevant.
- Instead of listing "task completed" as an accomplishment, try the following "task to complete code module xyz was completed within allocated budget. No unit test issues were reported and code quality was reported as high".

Future Objectives
- Define your future objectives in this section
- This section should provide a clear view of what you are focusing on next
- Again – be descriptive and address items which are relevant to you and your management team.

Issues/Risks:
- List all issues and risks
- Follow the format below or ensure that you address risk and issues holistically.
- Just listing an issue is not good enough. You should provide mitigation strategies, impact and status on mitigation.
- Escalate an issue when all mitigation approaches have been exhausted.

Issue # 1:	SME not available to support testing.		
Date: 11/2/07	Status: Closed	Priority: Medium	
Mitigation:	Review SME availability with team lead and plan appropriate participation on project.		

www.ingramcontent.com/pod-product-compliance
Lightning Source LLC
Chambersburg PA
CBHW081241170526

45165CB00009B/3139